'Passione' is a selection of the music moments that have accompanied my youth; a collection of cherished memories, of moments, of fleeting emotions, of sleepless nights.

Andrea Bocelli

A career is like a house: it's made of many bricks, and each brick has the same value, because without any one of them, the house would collapse.

Andrea Bocelli

A country that has really resonated with me and I was really impressed with was Israel. I found that the whole country had a very special atmosphere. I was there to perform, but it was one of the few places that I've visited over the years that I had some free time to explore, and I was hugely impressed by all the religious history there.

Andrea Bocelli

A love song must respect the canons of music beauty, entering the fibers of those who are listening. It must make them dream and pleasantly introduce them to the universe of love.

Andrea Bocelli

A positive frame of mind will definitely enhance your travelling experience. If I'm not in a positive frame of mind then the whole thing definitely becomes more of a challenge for me.

Andrea Bocelli

A voice is very intimate. It's something of your own. So there's always this fear, because you feel naked. There's a fear of not reaching up to expectations. As you become more famous, people come and expect to hear something extraordinary, so you don't want to disappoint them. I feel this sense of responsibility.

Andrea Bocelli

All that counts in life is intention.

Andrea Bocelli

An opera singer is like an athlete before a match. An athlete cannot overdo anything. In order to perform at the highest possible level, you need to refrain from activities so as to be able to express this power.

Andrea Bocelli

Apart from a period of crisis during my adolescence, when my voice was changing and I could not tame it - it was like a kicking foal that does not listen to reason - I have always been told I have a pleasant and recognizable voice.

Andrea Bocelli

Because I practice often with my children at home.

Andrea Bocelli

Because, in opera, I have to sing for people that are very far from me, instead of, when I sing a song, I try to imagine to sing like in an ear of a child.

Andrea Bocelli

Classical music and pop are two different universes, each with its own difficulties, peculiarities, depth and artistic dignity. In Italy, I think there is a fairly clear line of demarcation, but the history of music is full of fusion. Popular and classical music have always found points of contact, of crossing, exchange, both drawing mutual profit.

Andrea Bocelli

Criticism in good faith is good. When it's targeted solely to destruction, I'm not interested.

Andrea Bocelli

Destiny has a lot to do with it, but so do you. You have to persevere, you have to insist.

Andrea Bocelli

Even in the most beautiful music there are some silences, which are there so we can witness the importance of silence.

Andrea Bocelli

Every audience has its character; I like America - they love me. I suffer from stage fright, but in America not so much.

Andrea Bocelli

Faith has a role to play in life. It is not related to success. It is the other way round. Success is related to faith. Faith comes first.

Andrea Bocelli

Fatherhood is a very natural thing; it's not something that shakes up my life but rather it enriches it.

Andrea Bocelli

For me, riding a two-wheeler bike was very risky. Counting the pedal strokes before turning a corner and learning to hear the sounds coming from buildings, grass and the climbing frame made all the difference to basic survival and ensured that I didn't end up head-first in the sandpit.

Andrea Bocelli

For me, the most enjoyable type of singing is opera. It allows you to move, to wear a costume... to do something with your body. When singing in concert, you have to stand up in front of the audience, next to the conductor, which is less natural.

Andrea Bocelli

I also always carry my flute. It's very important for me to try to relax when I'm travelling, and playing my flute helps me to unwind.

Andrea Bocelli

I always knew I would sing. I just didn't know if I would be successful or not. But I sang at school, I sang at parties, I sang at church. Everyone always asked me to sing. I'd be playing football with my friends, and my parents would ask me to sing for their guests. I was never very happy about that because I wanted to play football.

Andrea Bocelli

I am a very lazy man, so, for me, the dream is to be at home on the chair with my family.

Andrea Bocelli

I am honored I have performed 'Quizas Quizas Quizas' with Jennifer Lopez, an eclectic artist who thanks to the charismatic power of her voice and to her soft sensuality, has managed to make this song particularly convincing.

Andrea Bocelli

I began when I was a child, because I was born and grew up in a little village. And many people ride the horses. So, it was a big - it has been a big passion for me.

Andrea Bocelli

I change the language with which I use my voice. In opera, I know I have an orchestra behind me; I have to communicate to people very far from me.

Andrea Bocelli

I consider the voice a gift from the heavens, and as all the gifts from the heavens, they must be used, but the minute that the heavens call it back then of course I will stop.

Andrea Bocelli

I did a pop album, 'Sogno,' in 1999. I think it's important to record another pop album because many people love pop music. By this kind of repertoire, some people can later discover classical music.

Andrea Bocelli

I don't have an extraordinary degree of self-confidence, but I know the gift I have been given from God and I try to share it with as many people as possible. Having a great voice is not a merit. I don't think it is a merit.

Andrea Bocelli

I don't have an extraordinary degree of self-confidence, but I know the gift I have been given from God, and I try to share it with as many people as possible.

Andrea Bocelli

I don't know if One Direction will stand the test of time. I have a niece who goes crazy for them. But the only way to judge art is to wait and see if it becomes evergreen. This takes a bit of time. Adele is a very good musician and I'd like to sing with her. But, again, time will tell if her music will become evergreen.

Andrea Bocelli

I don't like being called 'macho.' Macho basically means stupid and a real Italian man is not macho, he's smart. That's smart in both senses: elegant and clever.

Andrea Bocelli

I don't like crying. I'm a country boy, and we're the product of our upbringing. As a boy, I was told that men don't cry.

Andrea Bocelli

I first started playing in piano bars for three reasons - to make money, to be in the company of my friends - and also to hook up with young girls. I always knew, even before I played in piano bars, about the effect of my voice.

Andrea Bocelli

I have a European frame of mind and Europe is my home.

Andrea Bocelli

I have always felt an excellent rapport ever since my very first concert in Britain at Hampton Court. I have always felt understood. The British understand opera very well.

Andrea Bocelli

I have always loved music and singing, and I am open to listen to any type of music. Regardless of my mood, my heart is always set racing when I listen to opera. When I decide which music I want to hear, my choice is almost invariably an opera recording.

Andrea Bocelli

I have always tried to perform the music I love, and I think I am lucky because my preferences are often the ones of the public.

Andrea Bocelli

I have big, big stage fright.

Andrea Bocelli

I have had the good fortune of being able to sing with many of the finest voices in the world, and for someone who loves voices as I do, this is an enormous privilege.

Andrea Bocelli

I have to face life with a newly found passion. I must rediscover the irresistible will to learn, to live and to love.

Andrea Bocelli

I have trouble with modern art. But in general, all art forms fascinate me - art is the way human beings express what we can't say in words.

Andrea Bocelli

I know that my passion is for opera, but sometimes I like also to sing songs, because there are many beautiful melodies.

Andrea Bocelli

I like reading... French, Russian classics - Gogol, Tolstoy, Dostoyevsky, Flaubert. I also like Hemingway, Virginia Woolf.

Andrea Bocelli

I like to windsurf and ski, and most of all I love to ride horses. The wilder and faster the better! If I'm presented with a fast horse or a fast boat, I still get that shiver of excitement and I cannot resist. Luckily I never seem to have any accidents, and thank God for that.

Andrea Bocelli

I like very much to ride horses. I like soccer, I have had a passion for boxing since I was a child, although it would be stupid for me to box.

Andrea Bocelli

I listen to music every day for study reasons, and I confess that I have very little knowledge of what is going on in the hit parades around the world. I have no prejudices for any kind of music genre, and I listen with pleasure to many songs on the radio that my children already know of by heart, while I hear them practically for the first time.

Andrea Bocelli

I live for my children, so my number one rule is I won't go away from home for more than two weeks.

Andrea Bocelli

I love eating shabu-shabu in Japan - a kind of beef hotpot. But if you're talking about authentic, traditional food, then Italian cooking is one of the best in the world.

Andrea Bocelli

I loved playing football. In this particular match the ball happened to hit my right eye, the only one which I could see light and colour with.

Andrea Bocelli

I loved riding bikes and horses. I was eight when I started having lessons, and when my father bought me my own horse I couldn't wait to go off on my own.

Andrea Bocelli

I never think about gifts. It's enough to have my family present.

Andrea Bocelli

I prefer to work for my country in a free and independent way. I was born free, and I want to die free. I am always suspicious of ideology. Instead, I respect men with ideas.

Andrea Bocelli

I respect very much my public and also the music I perform.

Andrea Bocelli

I speak to God every day.

Andrea Bocelli

I started as a lyrical singer. But it was through the pop universe that I reached international fame.

Andrea Bocelli

I studied to be a lawyer, and after that I did something, obviously, completely different. With change, you learn something. If you do the same thing over and over again, you never learn anything.

Andrea Bocelli

I think I don't want to use drugs or medicine, so nothing. The only way is to go on stage and to hope.

Andrea Bocelli

I try to find some time for my horses. I began when I was a child, because I was born and grew up in a little village. And many people ride the horses. So, it was a big - it has been a big passion for me.

Andrea Bocelli

I want to have time for myself, my family and my friends. It's important because in order to sing well, you must have inspiration, and inspiration comes from life, from living.

Andrea Bocelli

I was a daredevil before, and after I lost my sight I was the same. I loved riding bikes, scooters and horses. I even learned to box. Muhammad Ali is my hero.

Andrea Bocelli

I was an agnostic until I realized that I had to choose between God and fate. The idea that humanity and nature are the result of fate was not convincing at all. I find the presence of God everywhere.

Andrea Bocelli

I'm a country boy, and we're the product of our upbringing. As a boy, I was told that men don't cry.

Andrea Bocelli

I'm most impressed by the Russian writers, so I love reading the works of Tolstoy and Dostoyevsky. Another author who has informed the way I think is the French philosopher, Blaise Pascal.

Andrea Bocelli

I'm quite shy, so I hate seeing my private life splashed over the papers.

Andrea Bocelli

I've always been on the side of science that tries to help man. I play an active part with the foundations I'm involved in. Science gives hope. If it were offered to me? Never say never. But I wouldn't kill or steal to have my sight. My blindness doesn't define my life.

Andrea Bocelli

I've always been on the side of science that tries to help man. I play an active part with the foundations I'm involved in. Science gives hope.

Andrea Bocelli

I've always known that I was born to sing, ever since I was a child.

Andrea Bocelli

I've been to almost every country in the world, and the most frustrating thing for me has been that my schedule has always been so busy that there's so little time before and after performances to explore where I'm visiting.

Andrea Bocelli

If you have a great love of singing, supported by others' fondness for your voice, then it is worth making every effort, of making every sacrifice, to achieve your goal. A great voice will easily find teachers who are willing to help a struggling young talent, and the ways of the Lord are infinite.

Andrea Bocelli

In essence, I set myself the objective of doing what I feel is right without having any ambition.

Andrea Bocelli

In my iPod, there are many operas, from A to Z. I have 'Aida' and 'Boheme' and 'Butterfly' and 'Cavalleria'. My passion is for opera, but when I'm in the car, I listen to everything.

Andrea Bocelli

In preparing my thesis, I have had the pleasure of collecting testimonies from colleagues such as Placido Domingo but also from singing teachers and musicologists. The entire course of study has confirmed what I already thought, that the value and meaning of opera singing, at the beginning of the third millennium, remain intact.

Andrea Bocelli

In singing, you cannot 'cheat' if you want to give emotions to those who are listening. You must have something to tell.

Andrea Bocelli

It is not Christian to go against someone. I am in favour of life.

Andrea Bocelli

It is the uninvolved parent who has to resort to strictness.

Andrea Bocelli

It's always beautiful to sing with other great voices. I like voices in general. It's a big privilege to have great singers next to me.

Andrea Bocelli

It's important for me who is at the table with me; the moment when everyone speaks to each other and everyone listens. If there's good food, it's much better.

Andrea Bocelli

It's true that I suffered a lot, especially when I was younger.

Andrea Bocelli

It's very important for me to try to relax when I'm travelling, and playing my flute helps me to unwind.

Andrea Bocelli

Let me say that I've never thought to conduct because the conductor has to think to the music before the orchestra. And the orchestra comes later. For me, it's terrible.

Andrea Bocelli

Listen to what others tell you about your voice. If you're only singing to please yourself, you might as well just sing under the shower. But if you're singing for others, you are reliant on them to ask you to sing.

Andrea Bocelli

Living is dangerous. The important thing is to know the limits.

Andrea Bocelli

Losing my sight had nothing to do with my focus on music. My passion for music was already there, so it would be a mistake to give too much significance to my blindness.

Andrea Bocelli

More people are listening to opera, and I'm happy - everybody must be given that opportunity.

Andrea Bocelli

Music is a prerogative of those who are willing to spend time to study it, understand and love it, well aware of the fact that one life is not enough to improve just one single note of what has already been written and performed.

Andrea Bocelli

Music is an art that goes well beyond science. Proof can be found in the huge amount of studies that have been carried out throughout the world based on music-therapy and the important results achieved.

Andrea Bocelli

My idol has been Franco Corelli. But every singer can teach you something.

Andrea Bocelli

My life experience has taught me nothing happens by chance. Even the idea of the ball in a roulette game: it's not chance it ends up in a certain place. It's forces that are at play.

Andrea Bocelli

My real passion is for opera. It was born and developed by listening to records, and my dream as a child was to record entire operas when I grew up, and this dream came true.

Andrea Bocelli

My style in Italian is very old-style.

Andrea Bocelli

Naturally, women are drawn to a man who understands the subtlety of emotions, and they know I'm a passionate man. But the reason I try to keep myself in shape is so I can sing better, not to look good.

Andrea Bocelli

Now I'm more sure and I feel myself more comfortable singing.

Andrea Bocelli

Often, I went in love with some friends in school. And, no, I suffered. Only later, things went better.

Andrea Bocelli

Opera is complex for those who perform it, but also for those who listen to it. It takes more time, more patience and more spirit of sacrifice. All this is well worth it because opera offers such deep sensations that they will remain in a heart for a lifetime.

Andrea Bocelli

Opera singing is in every way of inestimable value; a real heritage for all mankind that has been reached over centuries of studies, attempts, flights of the spirit.

Andrea Bocelli

People are often quite surprised by the sport and leisure activities practised by the blind. For example, tandem cycling is very popular.

Andrea Bocelli

People wonder if there is a relationship between my lack of sight and the way I sing. But there's no connection.

Andrea Bocelli

Popularity gets up people's noses. But I understand the importance and the function of popular music. There is an artistic purpose. Popular music helps people to develop a curiosity and leads them towards classical music.

Andrea Bocelli

Probably the first time I left Italy was to travel by train to Lourdes. I went with my mother and my grandmother - who was a very religious person - so it was a pilgrimage of sorts. I remember it as a very intense, but beautiful experience.

Andrea Bocelli

Singing provides a true sense of lightheartedness. If I sing when I am alone, I feel wonderful. It's freedom.

Andrea Bocelli

Some of us are born with a weakness for music. As a baby, music would stop whatever thought I was having. If I was worried, it would stop me worrying; if I was crying, it would stop me crying. Music was a healing thing for me.

Andrea Bocelli

Some years ago I gave a concert in the mountains with snow all around, and that was much colder.

Andrea Bocelli

Stage fright is my worst problem. A voice is very intimate. It's something of your own. So there's always this fear, because you feel naked. There's a fear of not reaching up to expectations.

Andrea Bocelli

Stage fright is my worst problem.

Andrea Bocelli

Success is related to faith. Faith comes first.

Andrea Bocelli

The activity of a singer that sings opera is similar to that of an athlete.

Andrea Bocelli

The fact that I am blind is not what defines my life. It should be of no more interest than my blood type. People wonder if there is a relationship between my lack of sight and the way I sing. But there's no connection.

Andrea Bocelli

The feeling of an evolution is a constant for every artist who is pursuing the search of refinement and enlargement of his/her own means of expression.

Andrea Bocelli

The most widely criticised singers in the history of opera, Maria Callas and Franco Corelli, happen also to be the best singers. I am honoured for being part of their group.

Andrea Bocelli

The nature of music is mysterious and so much so that it generates strong emotions within us. It moves along passages that reach the most intimate areas of our psyche without being tried by prejudices or influences of any kind.

Andrea Bocelli

The voice changes very slowly. I keep mine well under control and try with all my might to keep it exactly as it was at the very beginning.

Andrea Bocelli

The voice is something very mysterious. It's difficult to say what is inside a voice that moves people.

Andrea Bocelli

The world is full of many beautiful voices; I will perform with many of them. I love women's voices.

Andrea Bocelli

To be happy when you are travelling, you need to be happy inside before you leave. A positive frame of mind will definitely enhance your travelling experience. If I'm not in a positive frame of mind then the whole thing definitely becomes more of a challenge for me.

Andrea Bocelli

To sing a duet together means sharing with someone both the pleasure and the responsibility of making music for an audience which is there to feel enjoyment through music.

Andrea Bocelli

To sing a song is like whispering to a child's ear. It is an art heavily relying on improvisation.

Andrea Bocelli

To sing opera, one needs two things: the voice and the passion - and above all, the passion.

Andrea Bocelli

Very often, I recognize many, many defects, so I try to improve myself every day. I think my voice is very communicative.

Andrea Bocelli

What is beautiful enchants me. I mean not just physical beauty but a wider concept of beauty. There is beauty in poetry and in great musical or singing performances. There is beauty everywhere if you can just see it.

Andrea Bocelli

What is certain is that singing is not merely modulating a song by means of the voice: we sing and we celebrate the beauty that we can grow and live every day. If you want to sing and give emotions to those who are listening, you must have something to tell through your singing; you have to use singing like an instrument to tell something.

Andrea Bocelli

When I began singing, it was the first time I was happy in my life. As a baby, I would stop crying when I heard a great singer.

Andrea Bocelli

When I get on stage, my first goal is not to show my expertise, but on the contrary, to give a bit of happiness, of joy, of cheerfulness. I am firmly convinced that in order to sing well, you must love your neighbor and be passionate about life.

Andrea Bocelli

When I hear that young people have come to the theater for the first time to listen to opera, I'm very happy. Because it's the same thing that happened to me as a child. When I first heard the tenor voice, I immediately fell in love with this kind of music.

Andrea Bocelli

When I sing for myself, I sing in a more free, athletic way. When I face an audience, there is always some fear that makes me put the brakes on a bit.

Andrea Bocelli

When I sing, I think mostly about the music. But I know that, through singing, my body shows everything that I am. I am a very passionate man and I suffer a lot and have a lot of joy also. In my opinion, it is very important for me to find this stimulus and motivation for singing.

Andrea Bocelli

When I was very young, I started trying to sing like the great tenor Mario Lanza; my family used to play his records. We all learn best by imitating others.

Andrea Bocelli

When a little more than a teenager, I was a piano-bar pianist in the land where I was born and raised, Tuscany.

Andrea Bocelli

When the mood takes me, I like to be a man of action. I like to windsurf and ski, and most of all I love to ride horses. The wilder and faster the better!

Andrea Bocelli

When you sing and people want that you sing, then you can hope to be great.

Andrea Bocelli

When you're on stage singing, you're naked. Your voice is something very intimate, and that's why I'm scared every time before I perform. It doesn't matter if I'm singing for a king or a queen or the Pope, it's enough to be in front of anybody. I suffer, but I can't do anything about it.

Andrea Bocelli

You can be great only if it is your destiny.

Andrea Bocelli

You have to have great passion, because to sing operatic music requires lots of work. I study for at least two hours every day. The voice is like an instrument and requires constant exercise.

Andrea Bocelli